Victorian T

The story of the remodelling of the Duke of Bedford's fenland village by Samuel Sanders Teulon

by
Alan Edward Teulon

Illustrated by
Sian Catherine Teulon

The author apologises for errors:
Page5, para2 "eighteenth" should read "nineteenth" century
Page30 "162-164" should read "164-174"
Page54 "£22 per thousand" should read "£22 per hundred"

JEMA PUBLICATIONS

Published 2000 by Jema Publications

ISBN: 1-871468-09-4

Publisher's Note

Every care has been taken in the preparation of this book. The publishers cannot accept responsibility for any inaccuracies or for any loss, damage or inconvenience resulting from the use of this book.

Jema Publications
40 Ashley Lane
Moulton
Northampton
NN3 7TJ

The production of this book...

...was inspired by the late **Hugh Cave "Mr Thorney"**

...was assisted by the late **Jim Gregory**, Curator of the Thorney Heritage Museum

...was encouraged by **Margaret Fletcher** of the Thorney Society

Thanks are due to many other individuals and organisations who have provided assistance or advise along the way.

The late Tycho Wing, Agent to the Duke of Bedford at Thorney, who kept such helpful records.

Bedfordshire County Archivist, who gave access to records of the Bedford Estate.

Cambridgeshire County Archivist, who gave access to records of the North Level and Thorney Estate.

The Marquis of Tavistock, who gave permission to quote from Bedford Estate Records.

Lavinia Wellicome, Curator of Woburn Abbey.

Thorney Society.

Dennis Read of the Laceby History Group.

Cambridge and Peterborough Libraries.

Royal Institute of British Architects.

Institution of Civil Engineers.

Tony Noble and Karen Cropper for production advice.

Alan Bullwinkle, Hugh Cave Jnr, Renate Cave, Bob Fielding, John Kendall, Roger Mackett and David Scudamore.

Special Thanks are due to my daughter **Sian Catherine Teulon**, who produced the fine illustrations, and my wife **Christine Teulon** who has supported my obsession throughout, commented on all my scripts and has done her best to prevent me lapsing into nineteenth century English.

Alan Edward Teulon

"Thorney came as near as any [village] in the country to the ideal of a wealthy landowner understanding the economics of agriculture, a farmer master of its practice, a village not over-populated, with pure water, decent homes, allotments and a school instanced as the most successful experiment in social organisation that England has so far seen"

So states the Victoria County History of Cambridgeshire about the Fenland village of Thorney, situated about seven miles east of Peterborough on the A47 road to Wisbech. A village redeveloped at the expense of its landowner, the Duke of Bedford in the middle of the eighteenth century, to the advantage of both the estate and its inhabitants.

I discovered Thorney sometime in the early eighties on returning by car with my wife Christine from a break in East Anglia. We were immediately attracted by the varied terraces of houses on the north side of the A47 and then spotted the elegant tall water tower beyond them.

I had been researching the many works of my architect relative, Samuel Teulon, for many years and wondered if almost by chance we had stumbled on some more. He was recognised mainly as a designer of churches but I had discovered a great number of domestic works and the buildings of Thorney reminded me of some of them.

On my first visit I had no knowledge of this village, but clearly Thorney was a carefully planned settlement, probably part of a prosperous estate. So it transpired, but the estate office no longer existed, the village and adjoining farmland having been sold off early in the century. Most of the buildings were as built many years before and displayed the Duke of Bedford's monogram and datestones. I had to see if I could find a connection with Samuel.

An inspection of the appropriate volume of the "Buildings of England" series of books revealed no mention of an architect but referred to *"small but ornate buildings of mid nineteenth century", "Bedford housing in terraces" and "conspicuous water tower".* Samuel was comparatively little known and mainly as a church architect, there being and no comprehensive study of his career. However, about the time of our discovery I had aquired a copy of a recently published and exciting little book entitled "The Churches of S.S.Teulon" written by Matthew Saunders, an expert on architecture and a devotee of the work of Teulon. Although dealing largely with churches, the book did refer briefly to domestic work and had a section on Thorney, confirming our architect's involvement!

The link was made and so there began a personal quest to unravel the story of Samuel Teulon's connection with the Duke of Bedford and the story of why and how the village was rebuilt. This aim led Christine and I to make many visits Thorney and to Record Offices to search for plans and documents. Also to the taking of many photographs and the making of many friends among the residents of Thorney.

The Dukes of Bedford and the Thorney Estate

After the Reformation of the Church in England, the site of the ancient monastery of Thorney, together with the surrounding fenland, was granted in about the year 1550 to John Russell the first Earl of Bedford. The estate remained in the ownership of successive Dukes until sold to tenants in 1909 by the eleventh Duke.

The Russell family was one of the wealthiest landed families in England owning many thousands of acres of land in many counties, including large estates in and around Bedfordshire and Buckinghamshire, in the west country near Tavistock and also areas of London centred on Bloomsbury and Covent Garden. In the vicinity of the British Museum can be found Bedford Square, Russell Square, Tavistock Square and Woburn Square. Woburn is the location that most people currently associate with the family and where the public can visit the Abbey, the home of the Marquess of Tavistock, heir to the Dukedom.

Many marriages took place between the Russells and other prominent families and produced many notable people such as Lord John Russell who became Prime Minister between 1862 and 1865 and Bertrand Russell the famous philosopher and social reformer. Georgiana Blakiston has written a comprehensive history of the family entitled "Woburn and the Russells" originally published by Constable in 1980.

Francis the fourth Duke took a great interest in the estate and was instrumental in arranging for a great deal of the fenland to be drained in the early 17th century. At this time there was only about 400 acres of cultivatable land surrounding the Abbey, which was all that remained of the monastery. The massive drainage operations carried out in partnership with the King were undertaken by a labour force imported from the Low Countries in Europe led by a Dutch engineer, Cornelius

Vermuyden. This project cost the Bedford Estate over £100,000 and resulted in only partial success.

Further major works were carried out between 1827 and 1834 under the direction of famous engineers Sir John Rennie and Thomas Telford. In total the entire drainage of the fenland now known as the Bedford Levels is said to have cost in excess of two million pounds. The Dukes eventually benefited to the extent of almost 20,000 acres of land, more or less the entire Parish of Thorney, capable of producing some of the finest corn, vegetable crops, sheep and cattle in the country and in the early years resulting in an annual income of £10,000.

Throughout their period of ownership the Dukes of Bedford are said to have spent two million pounds on the Thorney estate, not only reclaiming it for agriculture but also improving the entire fabric of the village and improving living conditions for in excess of two thousand inhabitants.

Francis, the Seventh Duke of Bedford

Francis Russell became the seventh Duke, succeeding his father, in 1839 at the age of fifty-one years until his death in 1861 at the age of seventy-three. Much of his life before succession was devoted to politics and sports, particularly horse racing and fox-hunting and in mid life he was not subject to the best of health.

By nature he was not a man of good humour nor a very warm person, though he was said to be very hospitable. Perhaps this was because of a successful marriage to the easy-going Anna Maria Stanhope, a daughter of the Earl of Harrington, who bore him a son William, who was to succeed him.

Francis the 7th Duke of Bedford

When he settled at Woburn he applied a strong sense of duty, hard work and a determination to succeed in managing and improving the estates for which he now had responsibility, to the extent that he is said to have often risen at 5.00am in order to deal with estate matters. Georgiana Blakiston writes *"He bought, sold, built, drained and planted, with the help and advice of able men brought his property back from the verge of decay to be a pattern of good management and prosperity. Believing that the habits and morals of the poor would be improved by being well housed he built for his agricultural labourers cottages that were so convenient – even luxurious- that a country gentlemen being shown them exclaimed 'these are not cottages, these are villas' "*

At the start of his twenty-two year term as Duke, the Thorney estate was in a good financial state. This meant that some of the income, about £2500 each year on average, could be used for improvements, not only of an agricultural nature but more particularly of the village of Thorney, where most of the tenants lived, numbering over two thousand.

The Duke's Agent at Thorney

The improvements that took place in the mid nineteenth century could not have been such a success without the presence of a first class representative of the Duke living in the village in order to plan and oversee the numerous works and those engaged in carrying them out.

This man was Tycho Wing, born in 1794, who was descended from the famous mathematician and astrologer Vincent Wing (1619-1668) of North Luffenham, Leicestershire.

The Wings were a prominent family, including more than one eminent scientist, several military men and a number of parsons. Several members of the family served the Dukes of Bedford including Tycho's grandfather, John Wing, who was an Agent and his father John Wing who was Agent at Thorney. Tycho took up his duties in 1817, when he was twenty-three years old. His unusual first name is doubtless taken from Tycho Brahe the greatest naked eye astronomer of all time.

As the Duke of Bedford's most senior representative in Thorney, and a magistrate, he lived with his family in the finest house, Abbey House, opposite the Abbey. His wife Adelaide was the daughter of George Basevi a cousin of Benjamin Disraeli. Though based in Brighton, Basevi designed the Parish church in Eye, the neighbouring village to Thorney in the west, and the Fitzwilliam Museum in Cambridge. Adelaide and Tycho Wing had eight children, two sons and six daughters, several of whom died young, and none of them are recorded as having married.

The Thorney Agent was responsible to the Duke's Agent based at Woburn and during the critical years of the remodelling of Thorney; this was Christopher Hardy. At Thorney, Wing had reporting to him, a Samuel Bellamy, Surveyor and Clerk of Works and John Bradshaw, who was described in the village Directory as an *"overlooker of drains, droves and plantations"*. John Buck sometimes served as his Clerk. As well as his estate responsibilities Wing also had substantial duties in relation to the North Level Drainage Board.

Abbey House, where Tycho Wing lived

Wing's letters recorded in the Bedford Estates documents reveal a well educated man, of integrity and industry coupled with a thoughtful sensitivity not only to the needs of the estate but to its tenants. He demanded the highest standards from those employed on contract to the estate and did not suffer fools gladly. His letters were well composed and showed great attention to detail and remain a vital record of this important period in the history of Thorney.

Why Thorney was rebuilt

In 1848 a new Public Health Act became law throughout the land as a result of the government's growing anxiety about the circumstances of poverty and misery in Britain, largely in the cities and towns, but extending to rural areas too.

There was a growing awareness among landowners of these problems and the poor conditions in which their labouring tenants and their families lived. At this time most all rural tenants lived in small, damp, dark, insanitary cottages which were too hot in summer and too cold in winter. They were usually overcrowded and without a clean water supply, toilets, waste disposal, food storage area and lacking in any privacy for the sick or women in childbirth.

A contributor to the *Agricultural Gazette* in 1853 wrote about the effects of living in such circumstances.

"Home has no attractions for the young labourer. When he goes there, tired and chilly, he is in the way among domestic discomforts; the cottage is small, the children are troublesome, the fire is diminished, the solitary candle is lighted late and extinguished early...He naturally, then, goes to the public house, where a cheerful fire and jovial society are found, and becomes a loose character..."

A few landowners had remedied these circumstances by building improved housing on their estates from as early as the previous century, but such landlords were few and far between. Remedial action became of interest to the *Royal Agricultural Society,* which was established in 1838 and of which Francis, Duke of Bedford, was a Governor. An organisation devoted to remedying the circumstances was the *Society for Improvement of the Conditions of the Labouring Classes*, originally established in 1825, becoming more influential from 1844, when Albert, the Prince Consort, became its President and Lord John Russell, the Duke's youngest brother, was a Vice President.

Albert was instrumental in having "Model Houses" constructed as an exhibit at the *Great Exhibition* of 1851.

PLAN ·

OF·THE·

TOWN · OF · THORNEY ·

IN·THE·

COUNTY · OF · CAMBRIDGE ·

THE · PROPERTY · OF ·

HIS · GRACE · THE · DUKE · OF · BEDFORD ·

SURVEYED · BY ·

S·S · TEULON · ARCHITECT ·

MAY · MDCCCXLVIII ·

Title of the town map prepared by Teulon, before rebuilding commenced

In his comprehensive *A Social History of Housing 1815-1985* John Burnett writes *"The model cottage movement generally had as its object the building of sanitary accommodation which would provide, by the standards of the day, adequate space for living, cooking and sleeping, with separation, at the least, of parents and children and, if possible, of the sexes. There should also be sufficient storage space for food and tools, and, externally,. a privy and a pigsty-preferably surrounded by a good sized garden".*

Tycho Wing had considered the living conditions of the Duke's tenants at Thorney for some years before improvements started. On 25 March 1843, while on holiday in Brighton, Wing wrote a letter to Christopher Hardy, which amounted almost to a proposal for upgrading of the entire estate. His proposals included a four year cycle of improvements to the agricultural holding including farm buildings, new arrangements for police and village lock-up and additional provision of schools.

His ideas concerning the redevelopment of housing in the village were at this time modest; he wrote *"...not very fast perhaps but sufficiently so, and without employing any additional hands"*. He referred to the local problems when building *"...dampness of soil and climate is unfavourable to the long duration of buildings"* and the *"paucity of natural materials"*. He made it clear that it was not his intention to provide additional housing but to replace existing stock, as he did not want to attract outsiders to the village who in times of poor employment might be a burden on the estate. He was also against the provision of houses near to the farms where some tenants worked. He wrote *"...solitary cottages about the fen at a distance from the parish church, and from the inhabited districts, and withdrawn from observation afford great excitement to profligate habits..."*.

Wing referred to what he saw as a priority need in the village.

"... there are about twenty cottages, besides one or two houses of rather better character, for which I think nothing is practicable short of an entire rebuilding. They are almost wholly confined to the street which leads out of the town to the Wisbech Road; and several of them are in every respect

intolerably bad, small, low, damp, ill built, dilapidated and without adequate of ground attached to them for health or purposes of cleanliness and decency".

Five years later, on 14 September 1848 he wrote *" I estimate that to get rid of the crowded, unwholesome and demoralising state in which the poor are now living in the town, we must build thirty new cottages..."*

These forthright views of Wing were brought to the attention of the Duke by Hardy and were the subject of more correspondence and discussion. There was a spur to action three years later when the owners of the village of Hilton near Godmanchester, in Huntingdonshire, became the subject of highly critical comment in the Times newspaper and drew national attention upon the situation.

On 5 November Wing wrote to Hardy *"...Of one thing I am sure, the reformation of the cottages must go on here or we shall be liable to figure in the newspapers not much more creditably than the parish of Hilton is now doing in the Times..."*

The appointment of an Architect

At the time of the decision to rebuild Thorney, an architect ideally placed to be offered the task was already carrying out work on the Duke of Bedford's estates. He was engaged in the reconstruction of the church at nearby Stibbington and rebuilding the churchyard wall in Thorney itself.

This architect was Samuel Teulon, who, although based in London, was developing a busy practice throughout England. Teulon's designs for the rebuilding of St John the Baptist, the Parish church of Stibbington-cum-Sibson, where Tycho Wing's uncle, Rev. William Wing, was the vicar, were approved in November 1847.

At the same time consideration was given to the rebuilding of the churchyard wall and gates at Thorney. During discussion and the ensuing correspondence about the wall, Wing and Teulon had the opportunity to appraise each other's skills and attitudes and they clearly developed respect for each other and concluded that they could be successful in working together. Their frequent letters to each other are cordial as well as businesslike, often briefly referring to the welfare of their families.

By the time of his retention by the estate, Teulon had carried out a number of works, in London and throughout the country, of both ecclesiastical and a domestic nature. The Duke of Bedford appears to have been the first of many clients of the major land owning class from whom he was later to gain so many commissions.

In the summer of 1848 Wing and Teulon travelled to Woburn where the provision of improved cottages for Duke's tenants was underway. On 5 June Wing wrote to Hardy:

"Mr Teulon and I had a long day at Woburn on Friday and accompanied by Mr Hacker we saw the new cottages at Woburn, Millbrook and Ampthill.

I need not say that we were very much pleased; but I must add that my notions of cottage architecture in its most approved form have been considerably expanded and I have no doubt that when I come to settle the plans for improvements here, I shall derive great benefit and assistance from what I have seen at Woburn.

I am very glad that I went. Mr Teulon was also very struck with everything he saw at Woburn, and will I think do his part of the work all the better for it here... I expect Mr Teulon to come to Thorney before I have to return to London, and we shall then set vigorously to work in preparing for the requisite improvements here."

Samuel Sanders Teulon

Samuel Sanders Teulon, the architect of the new Thorney, was born on 2 March 1812 at Greenwich, near London, the eldest son of Samuel Teulon and Louisa Sanders. The Teulon family is descended from Antoine Teulon, a Huguenot Refugee, who arrived from France in 1689. Samuel spent a year at the Royal Academy Art School at the age of eighteen, followed by some years in the offices of two London builders. He set up his own London based practice in 1838 and won a competition in1840 to design almshouses for a the Worshipful Company of Dyers. He was elected a Fellow of the Royal Institute of British Architects in 1842 and was also a member of the Ecclesiological Society to whose Committee he often presented for approval his designs for churches and associated buildings.

S. S. Teulon
Architect

About half of Teulon's commissions were for the Church of England. He also carried out a great deal of work in his thirty three year long practice for members of the landed gentry, Members of Parliament and the Crown at Royal Windsor and elsewhere. He considered that his greatest church was St Stephen's at Hampstead built at the end of his life opposite his family home. His many works include over a hundred churches, about half as many each of parsonages, schools and houses, many cottage groups, five complete villages and many minor works. His great houses included Bestwood Lodge, built near Nottingham for the Duke of St Albans, Shadwell Court near Thetford for the Buxton family, Tortworth Court near Gloucester for the Earl of Ducie and Elvetham Hall in Hampshire for Lord Calthorpe.

S S Teulon was one of a dozen or so busy architects in the period of architectural design generally referred to as Gothic Revival. While Teulon had and still has his critics, his work is always interesting and often exciting. However mundane a commission might be, Teulon usually managed to introduce an unusual or eccentric feature. His many clients clearly liked what he produced and he worked for the Duke of Bedford in Thorney and nearby from 1848, when he was 36, until 1855, and possibly for several years more.

Thorney churchyard wall

Teulon was given responsibility for the reconstruction of the churchyard wall and gates at Thorney Abbey and work commenced in the spring of 1848. The builders engaged were Thompson and Ruddle of Peterborough. Teulon found some ancient stones with carvings on them, probably surviving from an early period when the Abbey was much larger. He decided that it would be fitting to mount them into the wall at the corner of what is now known as Church Street. An incident occurred which gives an early indication of the working relationship that was developing between Tycho Wing and his architect. Referring to the builders Wing wrote to Teulon on 5 March 1848.

Ancient stones, set in the churchyard wall

"They make difficulty about inserting the old stone with figures in the corner of the wall, as you proposed, but I told Thompson your orders must be obeyed and that if there was any difficulty he must write to you for instructions. I shall take further care to impress upon him and Ruddle that they are to take their orders from you, and from no one else, it is a necessary to start right in this respect".

The boundary wall of the Abbey has been repaired a number of times since its construction, the most recent occasion being in 1994 when the project was undertaken by John Wilkinson RIBA MRTPI, whose father had been connected with a firm, surviving from the nineteenth century partnership of Thompson and Ruddle. This latest repair was made possible by a grant from the Heritage Lottery Fund.

Designs for the cottages are prepared

Teulon prepared designs for cottages at Thorney during the summer of 1848 and submitted them to Wing, who in turn sent them to Woburn for comment.

Wing wrote to Hardy 14 September 1848
"I send you herewith some designs of Mr Teulon's, of which I request your consideration, not so much as to details, as in respect of their general character and fitness for adoption at Thorney. Mr Teulon is to come to Thorney to go deliberately with me into the entire subject of our proposed enlargements and improvements here on Mon 10th of October and before that period you will perhaps be able to form your own opinion about the plans and submit them to the Duke and return them to me with his and your opinions and advice respecting them".

Eroded stone with remains of the Bedford arms and date of first cottages

Wing duly received detailed comments from Woburn, and these were passed to Teulon who in turn responded with his own comments and explanations. Attention was given to such items as passages between cottages, room dimensions, number and location of fireplaces, light and ventilation, choice of single or double porches, and internal or external privies and offensive smells arising therefrom. In the considerations reference was made to the specifications of the *Society for the Improvement of Conditions of the Labouring Classes.*

Wing concluded in a report "... *it is suggested in the first instance to build twelve contiguous cottages on the Wisbech Road, at the end of the village, on a field now in the ownership of the Rev J Cautley which may be taken for the purpose... the intention is to remove to these the inhabitants of some of the worst cottages in the town, then to pull the latter down and build upon their sites some better houses for mechanics and small tradesmen... thirty houses at the least in the town are unfit to be maintained".*

Wing decided not to build all the cottages on the same plan, but to try some larger than others so as to accommodate different sized families. He arranged for a draft contract with Samuel Teulon to be prepared by the estate solicitors, Messrs Wing and DuCane, and the first group of cottages, fifteen in number, were completed in 1849.

One of the fine windows in the cottages of 1849

Estate cottages
Great landowners like the Duke of Bedford, whose estates were scattered over many parts of the country, adopted a common estate style that was widely publicised in the architectural and agricultural press. The Bedford cottages all contained two ground floor rooms - a kitchen provided with a cooking range and a scullery containing a copper - and either two or three bedrooms, one of them fitted with a fireplace; there were outbuildings including a WC, and an oven common to each block of cottages. Built of 9in brick walls, the cottages cost in mid-century £90-£100 each and, let at 1s-1s 6d a week, claimed to show a profit of 3%. They probably represented the most economic building costs, for the Duke had virtually organised mass-production methods, keeping a hundred workmen permanently employed and making windows, doors, staircases and fittings to standard patterns.

From "A Social History of Housing" by John Burnett.

The Duke visits Thorney

Wing was very disappointed that the Duke had not visited Thorney in 1848 and looked forward to an early visit in the following year.

On 25 January 1849 he wrote to Hardy *" I shall be very glad if the Duke can come to Thorney... that he may see if he likes the general character and spirit of Teulon's works, there is enough done for that but when the twelve cottages are built, we shall be committed a long way, as succeeding ones must in some aspects be made to correspond with them."*

Travel to Thorney in the mid nineteenth century

When Teulon made his regular visits to Thorney to meet with Wing and to inspect buildings under construction he was able to use the new and exciting form of transport that had was recently become available.

The Midlands were well provided with the railway at a comparatively early date. The important London to Birmingham route was opened in 1838, with a connection from Blisworth to Northampton in the same year. In 1845 the railway from Northampton to Peterborough was operating. The main line from King's Cross, London to Peterborough was not completed until 1850.

On 3 October 1848 Wing wrote to Hardy explaining that Teulon's plans had been delayed because *" the railroad between Northampton and Peterborough has been submerged and damaged by the very large flood which we now have in the Nene and the trains have been wholly or partially suspended from running"*

The Duke also made use of the railway as in November 1846 Woburn had its own station for connection to Bletchley on the London to Birmingham line.

For passengers alighting at Peterborough there was a horse drawn coach to Wisbech which stopped at the Duke's Head public house in Thorney. The railway from Peterborough to Wisbech, which passed through Thorney, did not open until 1866.

The visit took place in February and the Duke saw several projects on which Teulon had been engaged, including the churchyard wall, a farmhouse that was being improved and some cottages. On 16 February 1849 Wing wrote to Teulon of the success of this visit and that the Duke was *"charmed with Stibbington church"*, which was Teulon's earlier commission.

Wing wrote somewhat triumphantly to Hardy on 9 Mar 1849 *"I feel that the Dukes acquiescence in all that we propose to do at Thorney with regard the cottages is so considerate and generous that I have not a word more to say except that I shall do my best to spread my expenditure over four years"*. Clearly impressed, the Duke gave his approval to a four-year rolling programme of improvements, although he did express reservations about the ventilation in the cottages.

The Organist's Cottage

Wing declared his intention to make adaptations to the layout in the cottages for the particular needs of the occupants. However, he could not have anticipated the expectations of some of the more articulate tenants, for example, Albert Dawes who was the organist at the Abbey. He received a memorandum from Dawes written on 13 August 1849 outlining his requirements.

Parlour
Common panelled window shutters, whole to fold back each side the bottom part of window recess to be lined plain.
A common bound surfeet to top of recess. Architraves round window. Doorways and cupboard with angle bead to chimney

jam. A skirting round the bottom of the room 10 inches deep with moulding.
A neat marble patterned chimney piece of wood and appropriate Register stove.

Front Living Room
The staircase to be made of wood 3 ft wide in the clear.
The ceiling and walls of room to be plastered. A plain skirting round the bottom of the room and angle bead to the chimney jam.

A small kitchen range with oven and boiler.

Large Bedroom
Architraves to window and doorway and skirting round bottom of room with plain moulding.

Hovels
A small fireplace and copper (about 12 or 14 gallons) for washing purposes in smallest hovel, also window in each hovel.

The above alterations are absolutely required to make the cottage comfortable and suitable to its size.

Albert Dawes (Organist)
Thorney Abbey

Wing added a footnote:
"I have no objection to these things being done if Mr Teulon approves of them and will direct Mr Roebuck accordingly."

Hollow Bricks
These had been used as early as Roman times but were unusual until Henry Roberts, who designed for the Crown Estate and was Honorary Architect to the Society for the Improvement of the Condition of the Labouring Classes, patented his own design for hollow bricks in 1849. These were incorporated in the model cottages that the Prince Consort had built for the Great Exhibition of 1851.

Hollow bricks proved to have great advantages in waterproofing and insulation, as does the modern breeze-block. They also provided security from fire, deadening of sound, provided a duct for pipes and were more economic than ordinary bricks.

Wing and Teulon held one of their meetings in Louth, in Lincolnshire and Wing transmitted their views to Hardy on 5 November 1848.

"Teulon and I read carefully your paper about the hollow bricks. Teulon either concurred or anticipated all your objections to them and it seems quite plain that at present the idea is much too crude and too theoretical to justify them being adopted on a large scale of cottage building..."

More and more cottages

On September 1849 Wing wrote to Hardy with a list of works to be carried out by Teulon which included *"...about eight new houses intended for small village shops - tailor, barber, cooper, and so forth - and about fifteen new cottages inferior to those we have built this year, and containing some of them two and some of them only one bedroom each, to accommodate very poor persons with only small families or elderly and infirm ones with none..."*

The first houses built in 1849 proved a success, so Wing gained support from the estate to build a considerable number more in following years and most were built along the north side of Wisbech Road, although not located in date order.

The following list gives the dates of completion, total numbers of houses and the present house numbers.

1849	15	54 to 82
1855	6	30 to 40
1856	12	6 to 28
1857	8	86 to 100
1858	21	120 to 160
1861	5	27 to 35 on south side
1863	6	102 to 112
1864	7	162 to 164
1865	7	176 to 188

Cottage specifications

Written specifications for buildings in this period listed tasks to be carried out under the name of the tradesman responsible.

A specification might include: Excavator, Bricklayer, Mason, Slater, Tiler, Carpenter, Joiner, Ironmonger, Plasterer, Smith, Plumber, Painter, Glazier.

Gardens and Pigs

Each of the cottages at Thorney was provided with an adequate garden or allotment of land at the rear. Wing had something to say on this provision when he wrote to Hardy on 25 January 1849.

"The advantage of a garden to poor people is much increased by them having the means to keep a pig. I think the best course of all is so to plan the outbuildings in the first instance that a pigstie may be added if required but that it should always be built by the landlord on his own plan and that a small additional rent should be charged for it."

Early Thorney Schools

There was a school in the village before the rebuilding, which was paid for by the Duke of Bedford. Little is known about this school and about 1800 it occupied buildings in Abbey Place now occupied by shops. When writing to Hardy in 1843 Wing provided a summary of existing schools and educational requirements in the village.

Thomas Bellamy, was given £20 a year by the Duke to do the work of Clerk to the Parish and teach 20 boys reading, writing and arithmetic. In addition he taught another 18 boys and 8 girls who paid fees.

Bellamy's sisters kept a school for 30 girls and 5 little boys. William Bradshaw, who was also a surveyor, kept with his sister a school for about 45 boys and 25 girls. There were three other smaller schools with a total of about 40 more pupils and the Church ran a Sunday school.

Wing estimated that almost 200 children attended one school or another, leaving about 200 further children untutored, usually through their inability to pay. He was concerned at the poor prospects of gaining work by those from the village without any education. He was also concerned about the standard of teaching. As early as 25 March 1843 he wrote to Hardy " *The quality of instruction too, will require some circumspection; it ought to be of a sound religious and moral character; but not too exclusively religious, nor on the other hand so diffuse as to generate self opinionated and irregular notions and habits nor to unfit its recipients for the rough pursuits of a laborious life*".

Wing saw the most urgent need was for an Infants school and that he might be able to make available two houses, part of the old workhouse, for this purpose. He suggested that a master and a mistress might organise a school in two different parts of the parish.

Part of the new school in Church Street

The Duke was well aware that providing the children of his tenants with a good education would result in a better equipped workforce for the future; an important aspect of the village remodelling .

In January 1844 Wing sought a master for the new National School for boys in the village. The master would receive £50 a year and a house and would be responsible for about 100 boys between seven and fifteen years old. An assistant teacher would be sought from one of the existing schools through a merging arrangement.

National Schools were established throughout the country by the National Society set up for that purpose by the Church of England in 1812. The National School was rebuilt in 1875 and the building now houses the Ex-Serviceman's Club on the Crowland Road.

A new school designed by Teulon

On 4 September 1848 Teulon submitted a design for a new school for Boys and Girls and on 14 September Wing wrote to Hardy describing it as *"...more costly and showy than what we require... "*. Wing's requirement was for an infants school and a girl's school which were then held in *"very bad and inadequate buildings"*. He suggested one building combining both the required schools with a mistress house. On 31 December 1849, notwithstanding any celebrations for a New Year, Wing wrote to Hardy giving Teulon's estimated cost of a new building as £1,673.

The unusual horseshoe roof in the new school

Construction took place in 1850 with Samuel Teulon the architect supported by his preferred builder Robert Roebuck. In June 1851 the *"fitting up of schools"* was taking place. There must have been a grand opening event but so far I have been unable to trace any reference to this. These school buildings exist today; situated in Church Street, and now house the Library and Youth Club.

The Abbot of Thorney was once permitted to wear a Bishop's mitre. Was this why Teulon placed this figure on the school?

Wing's words to parents

With the National School for boys fully functioning and the new Girls' and Infants' School about to open Tycho Wing circulated a paper to all parents in Thorney. To the poorer parents he wrote as follows:

"Let me say a few words to the labourers and mechanics, and to others in humble circumstances. Your natural wish must be that your children should be enabled to maintain themselves in stations in life at least equal to, and perhaps a little above your own; at all events above the condition of the lowest description of labourers, but to do this, and especially as by far the larger number of children reared in Thorney must of necessity seek their bread from home, in more or less distant parts of the world, it is clear that they should have a good education, whereby they may be fitted to positions of trust , requiring skill, prudence, enlightened minds, good habits, and religious principles."

Thorney National Schools

Terms of Admission per week

Boys' Schools

Farmers' Sons..	1s 0d each
Small Tradesmen's Sons	0 6d each
Mechanics' and Labourer's Sons	0 3d each
For two of the same family.....................	0 4½d
For each additional................................	0. 1d

Girls' Schools

Farmers' Daughters................................	1s 0d each
Small Tradesmen's Daughters	0 6d each
Mechanics' and Labourers' Daughters.........	0 3d each
For two of the same family......................	0 4½d
For each additional................................	0 1d

Infants' Schools

For one child..	0 2d
For two of the same family.....................	0 3d
For each additional................................	0 1d

Schoolteachers

Some of the more prosperous families in Thorney chose to employ a governess to educate their children, but most sent their children to private tutors or local schools and had to pay fees.
The Census Returns for 1851 and 1861and local directory entries for years 1850 to 1858 reveal the following names of teachers employed in Thorney, although they were not all born there.
Maria Elizabeth Berry
William Bradshaw, National School
May Bradshaw, born Eye
Charlotte Granger, Girl's National School, born Walthamstow, Essex
Martha Ann Gunton, National School
Eliza Hammerton, born Eye
Mary Ann Johnson
Elizabeth Merry, Infants, born Spitalfields, London
Charlotte Waylett Newton, Infants
William Palmer, Academy
Edwin Pellow, National School
George Richbell, National School
Richard Smith, National School, born Darlington
Mary Goddard Wilson, National School
George Woollard, elementary.

Pupil teachers were recruited in Thorney, from as young as fourteen years. In later years more teachers were required as additional schools were opened at Wryde Croft (1866) and Knarr Fen (1880).

The new Post Office and Relieving Office

Teulon's involvement in the design of cottages and the school allowed him little opportunity to display his flair for individuality or even eccentricity, so he must have decided that an opportunity presented itself when he was commissioned to design a building required for more than one purpose. He produced his design for the Post Office and Relieving Office, and in a letter to Hardy on 14 September1848, Wing referred to this as *"...entirely Teulon's and may or may not be adopted according to the Duke's own inclinations"*. This suggests that, unconstrained by the recent specifications for model cottages, Teulon was hoping to do his own thing if he could get away with it! Wing clearly passed the decision to whether or not to proceed to his master.

The new building was erected on the site of the old workhouse and girl's school which were demolished for that purpose, cost £1185 and was completed in 1851. The building was put to a number of uses, not only Post Office and Relieving Office but also an Infirmary situated over the latter and also accommodation for a gardener and Police Constables. John Cook is recorded as being both Police Constable and Postmaster.

The location of the building is confirmed by a letter from Wing to Teulon 1 August 1850, which states *"I think the Post Office and all its accompaniments had better be covered with Collyweston Slates as it will correspond better with my Stables and House to which it is contiguous"*.

Sketch by Teulon of his proposed Post Office building

Another request to Teulon on 23 June 1851 was specific. *"The Infirmary over the Relieving Officer's Room here, requires a small outbuilding in which a copper can be placed wherein paupers and vagrants themselves can be washed and their clothes boiled before being taken upstairs"*.

> *" His Post office is Teulon's purest realisation of Pugin's dream of the idealised mediaeval world. It is picturesque to a degree with the Russell monogram, a royal coat of arms, a Virgin, and inscriptions on curly ribbons in a studious wrought asymmetry "*
>
> "The Churches of S.S.Teulon" by Matthew Saunders

The Duke's monogram on the Post Office building

The Workforce

The new building contracts demanded the availability of a large workforce of skilled craftsmen. There were insufficient living in Thorney so that a number of skilled people moved into the village and usually lodged with local residents. The census return of 1851, a busy period for the building of cottages, schools and the Post Office group, reveals the following:

Blacksmiths	2 from Thorney	6 from elsewhere
Bricklayers	8 from Thorney	10 from elsewhere
Carpenters	8 from Thorney	6 from elsewhere

Those from elsewhere often came from villages nearby, such as Eye, Wansford and Whittlesey. Others came from Bedfordshire, Northamptonshire or Lincolnshire. A few were from as far away as Manchester and Yorkshire. Two joiners were originally from Ireland and Scotland. A master builder, William Cave came from Wisbech.

Some may have worked previously on part of the expansive Bedford Estate, others may have moved into Thorney as employees to Robert Roebuck, Teulon's preferred builder.

The Contractors

There were three main firms of builders that usually made bids to carry out the building works. These were:

Cushing, who rarely won any contracts
Roebuck who carried out most of the early work.
Thompson and Ruddle of Peterborough, who were quite busy both in Thorney and on the Wansford Estate

Other men were employed as direct labour to the estate such as Clerk of Works Samuel Bellamy and his Assistant, his son, William Bellamy.

Robert Roebuck

He was born in Hull about 1816 and was about thirty-two when he took work in Thorney. His home at that time was in Laceby, near Grimsby, where the census listed him as a master builder employing a hundred men. He had worked for Teulon on churches and parsonages in that county. He was a nephew of

Stephen Johnson, a contractor, who also worked for Teulon in Lincolnshire. Roebuck played a key role in the rebuilding of Thorney although not always to the satisfaction of Tycho Wing who during periods when Teulon was in London or on other assignments in the country, kept a close eye on things. When the first cottages on the Wisbech Road were completed in 1849 Roebuck occupied one of them.

Roebuck was entrusted by Teulon to collaborate with Wing, and to use his initiative with the residents of the new buildings. In a letter to Teulon 11 July 1850 Wing writes on the subject of work being carried out on the "Rose & Crown" taproom.
" Roebuck is to my utter astonishment covering Simpson's building with tiles made in the field... quite unfit to stand the weather, I presume they are not included in the specification... He tells me that the tenants of the new cottages object to their walls being sized over as we propose because they all intend to paper them and he asked my leave to suspend the sizing and proposed to paper the cottage occupied by his foreman as a specimen".

The Behaviour of Roebuck's Men

As many of the workmen on the contracts in Roebuck's charge were not Thorney residents there was sometimes friction between them and the regular estate workforce under the supervision of Samuel Bellamy, Clerk of Works. Wing wrote to Teulon on this subject 18 June 1849 *"I have been very much annoyed by Roebuck's foreman, who has been quarrelling with the Duke's regular workmen and creating a very disgraceful drunken row in our streets."*

On 7 August he wrote in very stern tone to Teulon *"I am sorry to tell you that Roebuck's men have again been kicking up a shameful disturbance here. I have written to Roebuck, but if these proceedings are not put a stop to they will bring discredit not only upon Roebuck but upon you who introduced him here. I must beg of you to send me Roebuck's contract which I have never seen. I am strongly tempted to pay him for what he has done and to get rid of him and all his crew."*

To Roebuck, Wing wrote the same day *"I am sorry to inform you that your men spent yesterday in play and drinking and ended it with most violent and disgraceful fighting. I must put a stop to these proceedings at whatever sacrifice even if I close the works altogether. If you take work in the estates of noblemen you must not send men with the low and ferocious habits of the lowest class of railway workers"*.

Wing felt strongly about this matter and was determined to put a stop to it both in his capacity as representative of the Duke of Bedford and as the local Magistrate. Three days later Wing met with Roebuck and gave him a serious *"talking to"*.
Problems arising from the behaviour of the workmen probably occurred when Roebuck was away from Thorney on business for Teulon elsewhere, as at this time they were constructing parsonages near Louth in Lincolnshire, about eighty miles distant. No doubt the ale dispensed by one of the many drinking houses in the village was a contributory factor to the trouble between the men.

Recycling of Materials
Wing did not overlook the possibility of re-using materials when an opportunity arose, as was the case when some buildings were due to be demolished in Thorney. He wrote to Thomas Pear Junior of Spalding on 30 January 1850:

"We are going to make some extensive buildings at Thorney under the Superintendence of Mr Teulon, Architect, and for which Mr Roebuck, who built the new row of cottages last summer, will in all probability, be the contractor.

They are to be on the sites if the Old Workhouse and of the old girls' schoolhouse, both of which buildings with their appurtenances and some adjoining buildings will be pulled down.

They will furnish a great quantity of materials to be valued to the contractor and I have suggested to Mr Teulon who fully approves of my recommendation, that, if you will undertake the task, you should be employed to go over to Thorney, and make a detailed valuation of all such materials as will be suitable to be worked up in the new buildings, or be otherwise of use to the contractor."

Views of the tenants of the new cottages

It is remarkable to discover that in the mid nineteenth century a provider of housing for his employees would be so enlightened as to ask his tenants for their opinions on their new homes. This is what happened and the results listed by Tycho Wing to Christopher Hardy on 25 September 1850, about a year after the fifteen cottages were completed, make interesting reading.

Albert Dawes
The Organist at Thorney, two cottages have been formed into one for him. It is a very good one and he is perfectly satisfied and thankful.

Joseph Stimpson
This man and his wife and two grown up sons, with one daughter occasionally at home, were all living in a house with one bedroom, and all sleeping in it. The husband and sons were quite content to go into the new house but the wife who is a notorious shrew, disliked the change and did all in her power to disparage the cottages and to dissatisfy her neighbours.

John Hardy
A Master Bricklayer, he has been placed temporarily in this house, which is not altogether suitable to his trade; and another house is to be provided for him by means of the intended future improvements. Any remarks he may have made are to be taken as criticisms of the cottages with reference to their suitableness for labourers and their families and not as indicating dissatisfaction in his own particular case. His former dwelling was pulled down to make room for the Girl's School now being built.

Simon Green and William Colbon
These two men one the former a sawyer, the latter a bricklayer in the Duke of Bedford's employment at Thorney. They occupied a large house which had been formerly a Tradesman's house of

superior character but it was necessary to pull down parts of it to make room for the new schools, and to remove the inmates. They gain nothing by the change, perhaps in point of accommodation they are rather losers.

Benjamin Ashling
A working bricklayer, moved from an overcrowded house—perfectly satisfied and thankful.

James Smith
Servant to the Rev,d J Cautley having been brought by him from Bedfordshire; married and has a family, is satisfied with the house but rather dreaded the expence of entering it.

William Baley
Labourer with family removed from a bad house and quite satisfied.

Robert Roebuck
The contractor for the new buildings held by him temporarily for the accomodation of his foreman.

Edward Pope
Labourer removed to make room for the new schools, gains nothing by the change.

Catherine Cook
A widow 90 years old, has a man and his wife living with her, she also was moved to make room for the schools; gains nothing by the change.

Samuel Busby
Common carrier removed from a bad house and expressed himself very grateful for the new one.

Robert James
Labourer was living in a garrett of the old schoolhouse. His removal was a matter of necessity and he is understood to be perfectly satisfied.

John Gibson.
Gardner and agricultural machine man, was living with wife and numerous family in an garrett of the old workhouse now pulled down and is extremely pleased with his new residence and very thankful for it.

Tycho Wing added a note at the end of this report, which read as follows.
" It may be added that the buildings and population, before these new houses were built, were very much overcrowded; and that the dispersion of the population over a larger area is calculated to be of general benefit to the salubrity of the entire village".

Farmhouses on the Fen

In 1843 Wing proposed a programme of repairing or rebuilding all the farmhouses on the estate, over a four yearly cycle, with a quarter of the estates farms being refurbished each year. It was suggested that the tenants bear some of the cost depending on the degree of improvement. When Teulon started his contract with the estate in 1848, he was very quickly asked to rebuild a farmhouse on French Drove occupied by William Chettle.

Chettle's house was pulled down and completely rebuilt on what were difficult foundations. On 18 August Wing wrote to Hardy *" Ruddle and Thompson... are rebuilding here a farmhouse for William Chettle on a design of Mr Teulon's, which by the bye will be a specimen of his abilities in that way"*

On 14 September Wing wrote to Hardy about this farmhouse *"The internal arrangement consists of nothing more than usual, two sitting rooms, kitchen and back kitchen, store room, pantry, etc., and my only question to put to you about it is as to the external style and character; whether it is much as the Duke and you will wish to be adopted here on future occasions."*

An interesting query arose as the house reached completion. Wing wrote to Teulon 10 December *" You may without hesitation provide a soft water tank for Chettle but the question of the water closet I have referred to Mr Hardy, as it forms a precedent which may lead to numerous applications and which in the end to a very serious expence."*

The Duke approved of Chettle's farmhouse and as there were many more on the Fen, there is no doubt that Teulon's hand was involved in others along with their accompanying labourers cottages.

Water Supply in Thorney

Wing wrote to Hardy 5 August 1849 *"At present the poor have no water to drink except from the river water after pollution by the sewage from the town".* On the following day he wrote to Teulon *"The river water is often much impregnated with vegetable and animal matter and will never by its grossness tempt the poor into sobriety or manners".* As the fens were without springs the rivers had to be used not only for navigation and sewage disposal but also for water supply, washing and drinking !

If the conditions of living were to be improved for the poor of Thorney then it was necessary to improve not only their accommodation but to provide them with better services of which water was the most basic need.

Early consideration by Wing and Teulon settled on a proposal for a well on The Green in front of the Abbey and based on the design of one situated on the Duke's Buckinghamshire estate at Chenies. Both the Duke and Duchess became involved in this consideration, and received assurance from Wing that the expenditure of £100 was largely for the stone facing of the proposed well house or pump shed.

A report of 1848, giving observations on Teulon's designs explains that *"it was the original intention to adopt the best example of ancient conduits, such as at Glastonbury, Wells and Lincoln and this proposal was made under circumstances of there being a good deal of stone of the best quality available for the purpose removed from the Abbey Church when it was enlarged"*. However after several months of deliberation the proposal for a well was abandoned for a more ambitious scheme.

Writing to Hardy in the following year, on 21 September, Wing lists at the top of a list of improvements to the town, *"Drainage and sewerage and supply of water to the town"*. On 26 September he wrote to Teulon *"I have desired Roebuck to bring over with him ... an experienced well digger out of Lincolnshire in the northern part of which county they have great success in digging for water in the low marshes and I am anxious to ascertain if it be not possible to procure some spring water here instead of relying wholly on the river supply which will always be to a certain extent contaminated"*.

The Architect introduces an Engineer

Throughout his career Teulon, used the finest craftsmen and sculptors for his buildings and employed the leading specialists in the new technology of the day. His work in Thorney was no exception. On 16 October the ailing Wing wrote to Hardy *"I had three hard days work with Mr Teulon last week in examining the new cottages now nearly finished and arranging the ground details of all that is further proposed to be done in this town.... Mr Teulon brought with him an Engineer, a Mr Jones of 36, Throgmorton Street (London) whom he represented to be well versed in drainage and supplying water to towns. He has made a careful survey of the town and taken levels and made some borings of the adjacent high and low lands all which will in due time be reported...Mr Jones seems to have no doubt that a considerable amount of water for drinking may be obtained by digging on the high lands but he also thinks that water from the River Nene which he examined would afford a very palatable source of supply and I think will prefer this".*

Teulon's chosen Engineer proved a success with Wing as on 17 December John Buck wrote a letter to Jones on behalf of the ailing Wing.

" Mr Wing wishes me to inform you that your plans for Thorney are about to be laid before the Duke of Bedford, and that no steps can be taken till his Grace's pleasure respecting them is made known" The Duke's subsequent approval led to a great deal of advanced and lasting improvements to Thorney.

John Hodgson Jones was the young engineer that Teulon introduced to the Thorney Estate in 1849. Jones was born in London in 1823 and his career began as an apprentice to Mr T Doe, followed by four years as an assistant to Mr T G Barlow and three years with Mr E A Manby and he had just set up his own business at 36, Throgmorton Street in London. During the years prior to this first private contract, at Thorney, he gained a great deal of experience abroad, unlike Teulon,

Stamp of Jones the engineer

whose practice was confined to England. This work included gas and water works at Padua and Venice in Italy and gas works at Madrid, Valencia and Malaga in Spain.

Costs of the Improvements

A list of 8 January 1850 provides examples of estimated costs of some of the improvements

Engineering Works supervised by Mr Jones

Reservoir and filters	£340
Main Pipe with pumps to supply village	180
Tank upon Standards with temporary pump this to afford means of supply unless or until a tower etc are built	250
Water from the highlands to opposite Dukeshead Inn with all requisite appurtenances	397
Altering Peterborough Road Bridge	206
Quay wall opposite Dukeshead	111
Sewage	1,155
Subsoil and Service Drainage of Town	136
Lowering Wisbech Road in part of new buildings	64
Gas Mains	200
Total	£3,039

Costs of Building Works supervised by Mr Teulon

Schools	£1,373
Post Office and other buildings in the same group	885
Wheelwright, Tailor and Carpenter	1432

Fishmonger, Cooper and six cottages	1562
Mr Maker's house and premises	800
Simpson, Rose and Crown Public House	200
	Total £6252

These estimates were based on the bricks, stone and lime being supplied by the Duke. Were this not the case the cost total would have been £8,037, giving a total for Jones and Teulon of £11,076, a substantial amount, which Wing thought would occupy the estate until 1853.

Locally Made Bricks

Although the Nene Valley east of Peterborough is known for clay deposits ideal for the making of bricks, Wing used local sources of clay wherever possible. This was the case when the site for the reservoir associated with the works was excavated. In a letter to Hardy on 20 June 1850 Wing reckoned that there would be sufficient clay for Roebuck, as contractor, to make 200,000 bricks at a cost to the estate of 15s 8d per thousand bricks. The current cost of the cheapest brick one hundred and fifty years later, is over £22 per thousand, that is, nearly 300 times as much!

A Leak to the Press

As is so often the case today, someone involved with the ambitious plans to improve Thorney chose to talk enthusiastically to the local press before obtaining the approval of the agent Wing. The following item appeared in the Cambridgeshire Chronicle on 3 November 1849.

Thorney,-- The Duke of Bedford is about to rebuild the town of Thorney, upon a magnificent model plan at an enormous outlay; the works are to be completed in about three years. The plans and specifications have already been laid before him by an eminent London architect, and have received his entire approbation. The work has been commenced by the erection of 15 very handsome labourer's cottages, constructed on the plan communicated by his Grace to the Royal Agricultural Society some time ago, and they will be an ornament to his splendid estate, and a credit to the builder, Mr Roebuck, from the neighbourhood of Louth. Another useful work is to be commenced immediately, namely, the erection of a gas-house; and also a steam engine for the supply of pure water; the contracts are already taken. The Duke of Bedford is the proprietor of 19,000 acres of land in Thorney and contiguous parishes.

A week later, on 10 November, the newspaper printed the following.

We regret to announce that the paragraph in our last number about the rebuilding of Thorney by the Duke of Bedford is not exactly correct. Some improvements are about to be made and have partly been begun in the construction of 15 new cottages during the past summer but it is not proposed to carry works to the extent nor altogether of the character alleged in the last paragraph last week, neither have any detailed plans been submitted to his Grace nor have any contracts been entered into for future operations.

The Tank Yard

The works for providing services to Thorney were situated on a site which has become known as the Tank Yard. They were complex and advanced for the time, supplying gas and water and processing sewage, and must have incurred considerable expense, in further payments to both Jones and Teulon, possibly in excess of £20,000.

Water was taken from the Thorney River, purified, stored in a great tank at the top of a tower and piped to every house in the village, except those to be demolished and replaced. This not only provided water for domestic purposes but provided a ready supply in case if fire.

Gas was manufactured, stored in a gasometer and piped to all houses.

Sewage was collected and deodorised and stored in containers for sale as manure.

Power for these processes was provided by two **Beam Engines** manufactured by **Neilson of Glasgow**, which also operated the sawmills and carpenter's shop. The latter produced a considerable amount of estate fencing, as improved drainage of the fens meant that former dyke boundaries could be replaced with fences.

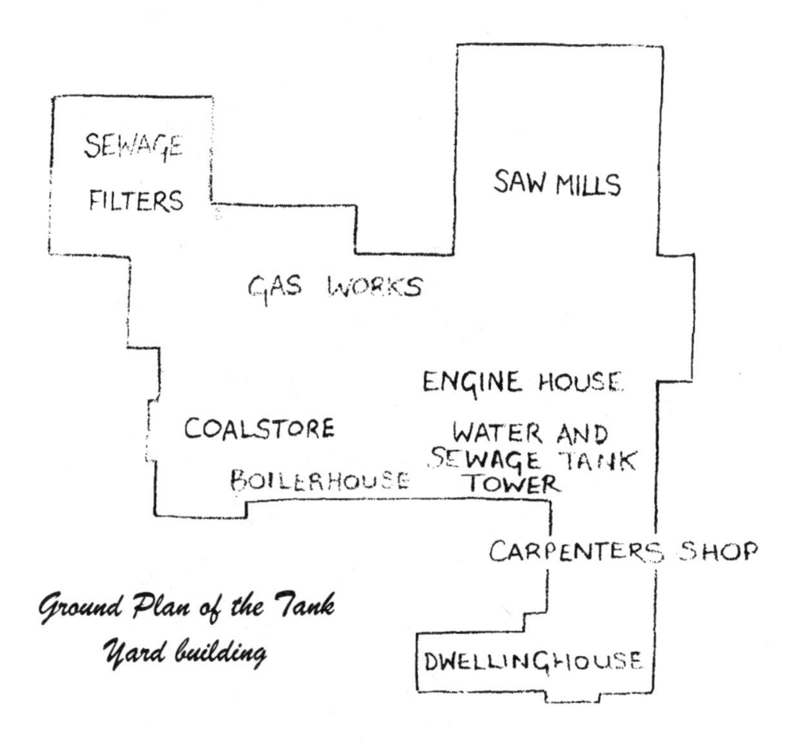

Ground Plan of the Tank Yard building

A dwelling house was provided for the manager of the works.

One of the beam engines by Neilson of Glasgow, which was installed in the Tank Yard building

The Tank Yard building and its great tower completed in 1855

Unpleasant experiments with sewage

Earlier attempts had been made to dispose of the sewage from the village. The Annual Report of the estate in 1855 reports that "To prevent the sewage from corrupting the water, shutting the sewers out from the river and connecting them with the dykes outside if the town, was first tried, but the want of fall in that level country prevented their contents from passing off and caused the dykes for more than a mile around the town to be filled with offensive matter, by which the water in them was rendered unfit for the cattle to drink and the air was made almost poisonous and the health of the town and its vicinity was greatly endangered".

From Tank Yard to Bedford Hall

After the Tank Yard was completed the works supplied the village with essential services which most people in rural England and sometimes in urban areas did not have for many years to come. It was not unusual for some of the greatest houses in the country to have primitive sanitary arrangements even at the turn of the century

When Thorney became linked to main services for water and gas supply, Tank Yard and its machinery became redundant. The beam engines and boilers, etc were removed in the thirties and disposed of.

The buildings had a variety of temporary uses during a period of over forty years. These included church services when the Abbey church was not available, entertainment for troops at the end of World War I, accommodation for Scouts, offices for local authorities, drainage board and Fire Service, and unusual community activities, such as trying on gas masks in World War II and schooling evacuees.

After the war thoughts turned to the need for a village hall but no action was taken for many years. In 1973 the buildings were taken over by Peterborough City Council and demolition was considered. There was a great deal of local opposition, which led to a determination to achieve the establishment of a community facility in Thorney.

Bedford Hall, with the buildings refurbished for community use, was officially opened on Saturday 4 April 1981 by Hugh Cave, Chairman of Thorney Parish Council. The accommodation includes a function room, bar and kitchen. The building complex also includes the Parish Council Meeting Room and the Thorney Heritage Museum.

The Works are almost complete

The following press article not only confirms the successful establishment of the Tank Yard complex and the services it provided but gives an interesting insight into the fen on which it was constructed.

From The Peterborough Weekly News and Advertiser
Saturday, December 27, 1856.

"The following description of the very extensive works which are now nearly completed at Thorney, by the Duke of Bedford, who is the only proprietor in the extensive Parish or Lordship of near 20,000 acres, may be worthy of mention.

The work was begun in 1852. In excavating for the foundations for the tower and buildings, viz, the waterworks, gas, etc, at 12 feet deep was found moor or bog, oak, sallow, hazels with nuts on them, bones of the hog, bucks' horns, cockle and muscle shells, etc. After taking off from 7 to 9 inches of the moor, the clay became very hard. The foundation of the water tower is 18 feet below the surface; the tower is 6 stories high, 74 feet to the top of the parapet, and the chimney 15 feet higher, sexagan, and finished with a lightning conductor and winding staircase inside, to the top of the tower.

There are two engines (each of 12 horse power) by Neilson of Glasgow, for draining sewage, forcing the water into the tank, driving a saw mill, etc. The town is splendidly lighted with gas, and every house in the town with a few exceptions.

Oak and other wood is frequently dug up on the estate below the town. That which is found in the gravel is very hard; that in the moor very soft at first, but becomes hard after being exposed to the action of the air, both will take a good polish. That in the gravel when burnt has the appearance of wood ashes; those on the moor, the appearance of turf ashes. The trees found all seem to have fallen from west to east".

The improved road bridge, with gas lighting, over the Thorney River

What happened to the key people?

Francis Russell, the Seventh Duke of Bedford was widowed in 1857, when his beloved wife Lady Anne died. The Duke continued to manage his estates until his death in 1861, completing 22 years as head of the family, in which time he gained a reputation for prodigious hospitality at Woburn. In one year a total of 1,129 persons dined at his Grace's table, 2,596 at the Steward's table and 8,217 in the servant's hall!

Francis was succeeded by his son William, who became the 8th Duke, but put the management of the estates in the hands of his cousin, Hastings Russell.

In 1909, during the time of the eleventh Duke of Bedford, Herbrand Russell, the Thorney Estate was sold, tenants being given the first option to buy. During their ownership, the Russell family was said to have spent about £2,000,000 on the Thorney Estate.

Tycho Wing, the Duke's agent at Thorney, seems never to have been in robust health during the rebuilding of Thorney and his condition cannot have been assisted by his conscientious and industrious approach to his responsibilities, not only in Thorney but as Secretary to the North Level Drainage Board.

The visits of Teulon put pressure on him. He wrote to Hardy on 16 October 1849 *"I had three hard days (for me) with Mr Teulon last week in examining the new cottages now nearly finished... we got through but not without the penalty of a severe cold from which I am not thoroughly recovered"*. He complained of the *"severe weather and raw state of the fens"* and took holidays in places such as Brighton, Filey Bay and Malvern. Writing to a colleague on 30 January from Brighton he wrote *"I have been suffering lately from a severe attack of my complaint"*

Plaque donated by the author and mounted outside Thorney Heritage Museum

By the summer of 1851 Wing's letters were often written by John Buck, his assistant, or Adelaide his wife, as he was too ill to attend to business.

On 26 December 1851, this great servant of the Dukes of Bedford died at the early age of fifty-seven, so was never to see the final fruits of his considerable efforts in Thorney. He was buried at Thorney Abbey on 2 July 1852.

Wing's well-connected wife, Adelaide, died at the great age of eighty-nine in Tunbridge Wells.

The new agent of the Thorney estate was Robert Mein, a thirty-eight year old Scot, who was selected from twelve applicants for the post. He remained at Thorney until 1863.

Samuel Sanders Teulon, the architect of the new Thorney, worked for another eighteen years after the completion of the Tank Yard building in 1855.

Whilst supervising at Thorney, he was also engaged on other work in the locality; at Thornhaugh and Wansford for the Duke and on churches in the Cambridgeshire villages of Benwick and Doddington. Further afield, he was engaged on the design of various buildings on the Royal Estate at Windsor and Sunk Island on the Humber estuary and also Tortworth Court, a major country house for the Earl of Ducie.

His career flourished and his buildings can be found in about two hundred locations throughout England. So far identified to his credit are 116 churches, 65 schools, 59 parsonages, 40 large houses, 5 entire villages and numerous other works. At home in London he and his wife Harriet produced 6 sons and 4 daughters. His eldest son Josiah Sanders, studied at Oxford University and became a Canon at Chichester Cathedral and Principal of the associated Theological College.

S S Teulon died on 2 May 1873 in Hampstead, at his home overlooking his mighty church, St Stephens. He was buried in Highgate Cemetery where a number of his fellow architects also lie including Edward Blore, who enlarged Thorney Abbey Church in 1840. Memorial windows were dedicated to Teulon at St Stephen's, Hampstead and another of his churches, St Mary's, Ealing. Teulon's practice ceased when he died and remarkably little material from his considerable practice survives in the family.

John Hodgson Jones, the Engineer at Thorney, having completed the task of providing the Gas, Water and Sewage Works at Thorney, used this important project to support his successful application for full membership of the Institution of Civil Engineers on 24 March 1863. He also submitted in his support, gas or water works, or sometimes both, at Wansford, Arequipa in Peru, Leatherhead, Malvern, Banbury, Bombay, Port Louis in Mauritius, Port Elizabeth, Bara in Italy, Trapani and Marsala in Sicily, Corfu, and Valetta in Malta.

Some years later Teulon introduced Jones to another of his wealthy clients, Lord Calthorpe, and he carried out water and drainage works on the Elvetham Estate in Hampshire. Jones was highly regarded in his profession and acted for many years as a consultant throughout Europe. He died, still working at the age of sixty-nine, on 1 December 1892 in Germany.

Robert Roebuck, the builder of Thorney cottages and other buildings and who was brought by Teulon from Lincolnshire, sadly died on 18 October 1851, aged thirty six, before he had completed his tasks in Thorney. He left a wife, Elizabeth, and three children.

Thorney in 1898

In "The Fenland Past and Present ", Samuel Miller and Sydney Skertchly wrote:

" There is however a village, which we would mention; the well built, clean and pleasant village of Thorney.... the greater part of the village has been rebuilt in recent years. The cottages are of white brick and substantial, but not of that rigid idea that he was entering a rural barracks. There are indications that further improvements in the village are contemplated, and certainly by removal of some old houses, the widening of part of the road and the extension of the row of trees, the spot will be rendered still more picturesque**. Thorney, is in many respects a model village.....**This brief note on Thorney may not convey to the reader an adequate idea of what the village is, therefore we say to any who wish to know more - Visit it ".

Thorney in 1996

In "Travels Through an Unwrecked Landscape" Candida Lycett Green, daughter of Sir John Betjeman, wrote:

" Thorney....is a lovely and little visited place which you might have whizzed by on your way from Wisbech to Peterborough. But I bet you didn't stop. If you do stop, this is what you'll find: one of the finest and most exemplary nineteenth-century model villages in England with a strange, high water-tower as its pivot and, on the other side of the road, a beautiful abbey-church almost a thousand years old".

Thorney in the year 2000

Thorney remains very attractive except for one thing; the desperate need for a bypass to take the very heavy and persistent traffic from the Wisbech Road, which bisects the village. This would permit the visitor, and indeed encourage more visitors to enjoy the architecture and charm of Thorney. Much of the historic centre of this "model village" is already a Conservation Area containing many listed buildings and warrants urgent action by Central Government in ensuring relief from road traffic in the very near future.

BYPASS THORNEY !

If you agree that there is a need for a bypass for Thorney, please write to:

Department of the Environment, Transport and the Regions
Eland House, Bressenden Place, London, SW1E 5DU.

Thorney Village- a lasting achievement

The remodelling of Thorney took place because of the vision of its owner the seventh Duke of Bedford who realised that well-housed and healthy tenants would not only have an improved lifestyle but would provide a dependable and committed workforce. Writing in 1897 about the great Bedford estates, Herbrand, eleventh Duke, refers to the rebuilding of Thorney and notes that it had a minimum of crime, no evictions and no pauperism.

The successful rebuilding was due in no small part to the qualities of Tycho Wing, the Agent, and the successful working partnership that he developed with Teulon, the Architect. Teulon was based in London and able to attract to the Thorney contract Jones, a bright, young and promising engineer. Teulon spent about a third of his working life attending to his contracts in Thorney. He left a variety of styles in his distinctive but varied cottages, his picturesque Post Office, his Gothic school and his robust Tank Yard building.

Thorney village no longer belongs to the Bedfords but remains very much as it looked when built, except for a widened main road with no trees but with modern trimmings such as street lights and television aerials. Much of the village has Conservation Area status with some grants available from Peterborough City Council to assist with its protection.

The houses are no longer occupied by agricultural workers and some of the allotments have been sold off. Now Thorney is occupied by people from a variety of birthplaces, with a range of occupations and workplaces. Very few old family names survive in the village. Some villagers belong to the Thorney Society and it is hoped many more will join.

The Tank Yard building, which provided services to the residents for so many years, and functioned as the "engineering hub" of the village now serves as the " social hub" in its new role as community centre.

When Thorney acquires its long awaited and much needed bypass, its residents can look forward to a quieter and less polluted life. I hope that they will realise the interest that a "model village" such as Thorney may hold for the visiting public. The Thorney Society has made an excellent start in this respect and publications and guided tours of the village are already available. Perhaps an opportunity will arise to acquire a cottage in order to demonstrate how life was in 1850!

I knew there was something special about Thorney when Christine and I drove through in the early eighties. It turned out to be not only one of a few surviving rural "model villages", but one designed by a member of my own family, interestingly a descendant of a Huguenot family, working in a village associated with Huguenot and Walloon refugees.

Sources of Information

Bedfordshire and Luton Archives and Records Service, at County Hall, Bedford, hold records of the Bedford Estates.

Letters, reports and other documents found under references R4/4140-4145, 4178,4194-7,4203 and R5/4123-9. Estate Annual Reports and other reports held on microfilm.

Cambridgeshire Heritage County Record Office, at Shire hall, Cambridge, hold North Level and Thorney Estate Letter Books.

Victoria County History of Cambridgeshire

Buildings of England *Cambridgeshire*

Pedigree of the Family of Wing 1886

Census Returns for Thorney of 1851 and 1861

Directories for Cambridgeshire of 1850 to 1858

Cambridgeshire Chronicle of 1849

Peterborough Weekly News and Advertiser of 1856

Agricultural Gazette of 1853

Ecclesiologist of 1855

A Great Agricultural *Estate* by the Duke of Bedford 1897

The Fenland Past and Present by Samuel Miller and Sydney Skertchly 1898

Fenland Rivers by Iris Wedgwood 1936

Villages of Vision by Gillian Darley 1978

Woburn and the Russells by Georgiana Blakiston 1980

The Churches of S S Teulon by Matthew Saunders 1982

The Life and Works of Henry Roberts by James Stevens Curl 1983

Social History of Housing (1815-1985) by John Burnett 1986

Travels Through An Unwrecked Landscape by Candida Lycett Green 1996

About the author, by the author

I was born in Enfield in North London, one of the eighth generation descended from Antoine Teulon, a Huguenot refugee from the south of France who came to England and settled in Greenwich in 1689.

I worked in Jamaica as a land surveyor for nine years, then as a planning officer in South Wales. I recently retired from

Northamptonshire County Council, where I worked as Head of Countryside Services for twenty-five years.

Since retirement I have had time to concentrate on a number of personal projects and the Thorney project was top of my list. My wife Christine has assisted me in this and we shall continue our quest to locate and record the many other architectural works of Samuel Sanders Teulon and his brother William Milford Teulon throughout England.

I have been a member of the Thorney Society since I discovered the fascination of Thorney.

Alan Edward Teulon MBE ARICS

Thorney Heritage Museum

A Heritage Museum has been established in the Tank Yard by the Thorney Society. Situated in the former dwelling house of the works manager, it holds records of and displays on the village and Parish, past and present.

Entry is free but donations are welcome. The Museum is open weekend afternoons between April and October. Groups and school parties can be accommodated throughout the year by prior arrangement.

Conducted tours of the Abbey and village are available.

The Thorney Heritage Museum was opened by Councillor R Perkins Mayor of Peterborough on Saturday 3 October 1987.

The Thorney Society

This has been established to encourage local people and visitors to take an interest in the past, present and future of Thorney. The society manages the Heritage Museum, promotes local conservation and environmental projects and organises educational and social events.

Details of Museum and Society can be obtained by writing to:-

Thorney Heritage Museum
Tank Yard
Station Road
Thorney
Cambridgeshire PE6 0QE